Foreword

Vito always tells me about, "friendship, myself, power, nature, the heart and LOVE". I try to understand them, but the more you think about it, the more it is as deep as the Universe.

However, he has a simple idea, even this is the eternal task of humanity, and he acts and leaves with a smile. This is him, Vito.

I used to lose confidence in myself. I met him at that time, he blew my mind. He told me, "You are the coolest and the most beautiful person in the world. So, you must have confidence. Create your own life and act like you want to be in your life. If you always have love, you are absolutely fine."

He suddenly appears and then leaves with a smile in your life.

This is him, Vito.

"Jessie Cool"
June, 2020

My Poems

If you've been following my poems so for, you would know who I am.
If not, t doesn't matter.
Because this is c new book with new poems.
Just like a new day is the beginning of a new life.

Although, some say that we only have one story to tell & that's "your" story.
Everyone has their own unique story.
No one has the same story.
Every story is different.
No one has "your" story.
Your "life story".
The "story of your life.
Because there is only one of "you".

Write your poems down.
Let others know about your story, through poetry.

"The Don"

This book is dedicated to all those people who rebel & protest the injustices & inequalities in this cruel society of ours".

— "The Don"
January, 2021

Contents

1: I'm Sorry
2: I'm Not Working for the Man (with thanks to the "Big O")
3: Without You
4: Energetics (Energetica)
5: The Alchemist (L'alchimista)
6: From the Darkness to the Light (de l'obscurité à la lumière)
7: When You Dance with the Devil (Don't Expect to Walk Away)
8: Exam Time
9: Nature (Et amor natura)
10: The Face in the Mirror
11: Feng Shui
12: Synchronicity (Unus Mundus)
13: Fascism (Fascista)
14: Road to Nowhere
15: You've Gotta Serve Somebody

Acknowledgement of Land & of the Traditional Owners of this Land

I would like to acknowledge the Gadigal people of the Eora Nation, upon whose stolen land I stand today.

I recognise that this land was never terra null us — the land belonging to these peoples was never ceded, given up, bought or sold.

I would like to pay my respects to Aboriginal Elders past, present and emerging, and I extend this acknowledgement to all Aboriginal and Torres Strait Islander people.

Dark History:
This Continent of Australia was claimed by the British Empire in 1770 by Captain James Cook.
His first action was to shoot an aboriginal dead from his ship, the *"Endeavour"*.
The aboriginals had lined up on the shore watching this spectacle unfolding before their very eyes.

120,000 years of continuous culture & civilisation would end that day.
In an instant, the universe changed for these people.
For they were defined not to be people at all.
They were defined as uncivilised creatures.
To be used as slaves.

The British colonised Australia in 1788, with the arrival of Captain Arthur Philip & the 12 ships full of convicts that made up *"The First Fleet"*.
They landed on the 26th January, which is celebrated as *"Australia Day"*.
First Nation Peoples call it *"Invasion Day"*.

There existed between 250-700 nations before the *"White Man"* arrived.
There were between 300,000 and 1,000,000 aboriginals living in Australia at the time.

In the last 250 years, First Nation Peoples have endured incredible suffering at the hands of the *"White Man"*.

They have endured enormous cruelty at the hands of their oppressors.
Removed by force from their traditional land
Suffered from introduced diseases they never had before.
Forced to assimilate into white culture & lose their own.
Forced into slavery.
Women were raped.
Their children were forcibly removed from their mothers & families.
They were later to become known as the *"Stolen Generation"*.
The desecration & destruction of sacred & religious sites.
Addiction to alcohol introduced by the *"White Devil"*.
Forcibly repatriated in Aboriginal settlements far away from their traditional lands.

First Nation Peoples did not have any rights in their own country.
In fact, this was no longer their country.
It had been stolen from them.
They didn't get to vote and until 1967.
They are still not recognised in the Australian Constitution.
No treaty has ever been signed between First Nation Peoples & The British occupiers.

These injustices have still not been resolved to this very day.

"The Don"
January 2021

Map of Australia
showing all the Aboriginal Nations Before 1770

Captain James Cook in 1770 claimed this land as "Terra Nullis" for the British Empire

Contents

16: Rich Man, Poor Man
(Are you a wealthy man?)
17: No Justice
(Nessuna Giustizia)
18: Do Not Let Worlds Collide
19: Outraged
20: Fear
(Paura)
21: Let's fuck!
(Scopiamo!)
22: Orgasm Addict
23: The Dance of Life
(La danza della vita)
24: The Dance of Death
(La danza della morte)
(Dance Macabre)
25: A Cry in the Wind
26: Let's Get High!
27: Perversion
(Perversione)
28: Forbidden Fruits
29: Flatulation
(The farting Game)
30: Lo♥e Yourself
31: If You're Gonna Smell, Smell Beautiful
32: I Like it Rough
33: A Good Life!
(Buona Vita)

Contents

34: Murder Most Foul
35: Lost Innocence
(L'innocence perdue)
36: Death of Innocence
(Mort d'innocence)
37: Déjà Vu
38: Game of Empires
39: The 3 Acts of Sex
40: Non-Violence
41: The Death of Humour
(La mort de l'humour)
42: Porno
43: The Thinker
(Il Pensatore)
44: Revolution No. 9
45: Existence
46: Fuckability
47: The Music Inside My Head
(La musique dans ma tête)
48: Desire
49: Imagination
(Immaginazione)
50: Poetic Politicians
(Politici Poetici)
51: Sex Bomb
(Bombe sexuelle)
52: Happy Days

I'm Sorry

I'm *sorry* for my mistakes.
I'm *sorry* for what I've done.
I'm *sorry* for the things I did.
I'm *sorry* for the wrongs on everyone.
I'm *sorry* for my lies.
I'm *sorry* for the suffering I caused.
I'm *sorry* for your loss of faith in me.

I'm *sorry* if I made you sad.
I'm *sorry* if I hurt someone.
I'm *sorry* if I was bad.
I'm *sorry* if I hurt you.
I'm *sorry* if I wasn't true.
I'm *sorry* if I screwed up
I'm *sorry* If I made you cry.

Sorry is such a simple word.
Sorry is so much more than that.
Sorry is about making one's peace with the things one's done wrong in their past.
Sorry is about making things RIGHT.
Sorry is about reconciliation.
Sorry is the HARDEST word.
Sorry is a BEAUTIFUL word.

"The Don"
10.06.2020

I'm Not Working for the Man
(with thanks to the "Big O")

I'm not working for the man.
I'm not going to lend him a hand.
I'm making a stand.
Because I'm not working for the man.

I'm not gonna pick up my feet.
I don't care if there's a deadline to meet.
I don't if you make it on time.
I'm gonna relax.
I'm not gonna give you my elbow & back.
You're not gonna see me from behind.

I'm not working for the man.
I'm not going to lend him a hand.
I'm making a stand.
Because I'm not working for the man.

So, I'm not pickin' 'em up nor I'm laying 'em down.
Cause he works me into the ground.
I sing my song, 'cause I've done no wrong.
I want to kill him & wouldn't that be right.

'Cause, I'm not working for the man.
I'm not going to lend him a hand.
I'm making a stand.
Because I'm not working for the man.

Well the boss man's daughter sneaks me some water.
Every time her daddy's down the line.
She says, "meet me tonight, fuck a-me right & I'll show you a good time".

I used to slave all day without much pay.
Now, I've got to say, "I'm ok".
That the time's all mine.
And I'm doing fine.
'Cause I'm fucking the boss's daughter.

Well, I'm not working for the man.
I'm not going to lend him a hand.
I'm making a stand.
Because I'm not working for the man.
And I'm having a good time!

"The Don"
12.06.2020

Without You

Do you think it's easy?
Without you.

It's driving me crazy.
Without you.

Life is not breezy.
Without you.

Don't think it's easy.
Without you.

Do you think I'm lazy?
Without you.

Everything is hazy.
Without you.

My life is going crazy
Without you.

I'm having dreams about you.
Without you.

I walk into trees.
Without you.

I'm down on my knees.
Without you.

Life don't mean a thing.
Without you.

You're my everything.
Without you.

I can't even dress myself.
Without you.

I haven't washed myself for months.
Without you.

I haven't shaved or cut my hair.
Without you.

I haven't left the house.
Without you.

I'm living like a mouse.
Without you.

I haven't brushed my teeth.
Without you.

I may commit suicide.
Without you.

I may even kill myself.
Without you.

I think that you're a bitch.
Without you.

For leaving in a ditch.
Without you.

I'll never get over this.
Without you.

Don't you know I'm a sensitive guy?
Without you.

Maybe it's for the best.
Without you.

I'll put it to the test.
And be Without you.

And that way put you out to rest.
Being Without you.

I'm now living without you within me.
Without you is within me.

Without you is the way to be.
Without you means I'm free.

Without you I can be
With or without you is the way to be.

"The Don"
13.06.2020

Energetics

(Energetica)

We live in a world of make believe.
Nothing is real.
It's all an illusion.
Nothing is as we see it.

It's all a mirage.
It's a trick of the light.
It's playing with our senses.
It's playing havoc with our sight.

"I think, therefore I am!"
Said a great man.
But my thinking is not real.
So therefore, I am not.

It's done with light & mirrors.
Like the illusionists of times gone by.
It's all empty space.
We're not even in the race.

Matter doesn't exist, you know.
It's a trick of the eye.
We see what we want to see.
And disregard the rest.

We exist in empty space.
In the vastness of the great unknown.
In the unfathomable emptiness of Space-Time.
The infinite cosmic expanse of paradoxes.

A place where all Gods are dead.
There's no place for them here.
A place with no beginning & no end.
Where limits have no meaning.

A place where there is no birth or death.
These are just mortal concepts.
They have no place or purpose here.
Here in the Nothingness & the Everythingness!

A place where dualities exist side by side.
Where opposites attract & repel.
Where up & down exist in the same time & place.
Where time & place has no meaning.

A place where the meaningless has meaning.
A place where Nothing exists & Everything exists
All at the same time.
A place where you don't need your mind.

A place where confusion & clarity make complete sense.
A place where Sense & Non-sense is understandable.
A place that exists outside anything we've ever imagined.

A place where the physical & the metaphysical coexist.
Where the two are intertwined.
One can be the other at any given time.
A place where all that exists is Energy!

Energetics

(Energetica)

"The Don"
13.05.2020

The Alchemist
(L'alchimista)

Wanna be a magician?
Wanna do miracles?
Wanna turn water into wine?
Wanna turn lead into gold?

Wanna seek the treasure?
Wanna find the holy grail.
Wanna touch the sublime?
Wanna touch the spiritual?

Wanna see the unseen?
Wanna know the unknown?
Wanna imagine the unimaginable?
Wanna see into the abyss?

Wanna know the answers to all your questions?
Wanna the questions to all your answers?
Wanna see into pool of forever?
Wanna go beyond the unknown?

Wanna look into your heart?
Wanna look into your soul?
Wanna look into the darkness?
Wanna live forever?

Wanna see into the darkness?
Wanna meet your maker?
Wanna meet the grim reaper?
Wanna meet your death?

Wanna see your future?
Wanna move through time & space?
Wanna cheat your death?
Wanna be a God?

"The Don"
13.06.2020

From the Darkness to the Light

(de l'obscurité à la lumière)

This is what our struggle is all about.
To reach that eternal flame.
To seek that brightest light.
To climb up those stairs.
To follow the blowing wind.
To swim the eternal river.
To walk across the dessert.
To cross dusty plains.
To breath that fresh clean air.
To fly into the sky without a care.
To emerge from the murky depths.
To sleep beneath the stars.
To awaken from your sleep.
To awaken from you slumber.
To follow your unfilled dreams.
To shallow your shallow pride.
To forgive you enemies.
To persevere along your journey.
To never give up until the end.
To never your faith in yourself & others.
To never be tempted by fake rewards.
To never be lured by hollow words of praise.
To be strong & not be persuaded by figures from the depths.
To stand naked, alone & proud.
To stand before your maker.
To say, "I have arrived!"
To stand your ground.
To sit upon the chair.
To have at your destination.
To have finally reached The End.
To have completed your long, arduous journey.
From the Darkness to the Light.

"The Don"
13.06.2020

When You Dance with the Devil
(Don't Expect to Walk Away)

Made an arrangement with someone you trust?
Do you have a deal going down?
I hope you've chosen the right guy.
I hope you haven't made a mistake.
'Cause, when you dance with the Devil, don't expect to walk away.

I hope you know what you're doing here.
I hope you know whom you are dealing with.
I hope you know what's going down.
I hope you you've got the right man.
'Cause, when you dance with the Devil, don't expect to walk away.

Have you signed a contract yet?
Have you done your research?
Have you read the fine print?
Have you checked it over thoroughly?
'Cause, when you dance with the Devil, don't expect to walk away.

There is still time to back out of this.
There is still time to walk away.
There is still time not to make this deal.
There is still time not to go through with it.
'Cause, when you dance with the Devil, don't expect to walk away.

The deal that you make can never be broken.
The contract you sign is signed with you blood.
The arrangements you make do not have an expiry date
The dance that you start can never be stopped.
The dance that you start does not have an end.
'Cause, when you dance with the Devil, don't expect to walk away.

"The Don"
13.06.2020

Exam Time

I hate tests.
I hate quizzes.
I hate being rated.
I hate Exam Time

Maybe it's the stress?
Maybe it's the pressure?
Maybe it's competition?
I hate Exam Time?

I still have nightmares.
I still get sweaty palms.
I still feel anxiety
I hate Exam Time.

I always studied hard.
I always tried my best.
I always to do well in tests.
I hate Exam Time

It made very competitive.
It made me want to be the best.
I made me want to beat the rest.
I hate Exam Time

It made me into a perfectionist.
It made work very hard.
It made me seek rewards.
I hate Exam Time

I was told they were important.
I was told they were necessary.
I was told they were for my Future.
I hate Exam Time

It was one big lie.
It was one big joke.
It was on big "crok-of-shit"!
I hate Exam Time.

Competition is not good for anyone.
Being rated & classified.
Being assessed & categorised.
I hate Exam Time.

I am who I am.
I don't need to be examined.
I don't to validate myself to anyone.
I hate Exam Time.

I don't need to prove myself to you or anyone.
I don't need to be judged by someone else.
I don't need to fit into a System.
Created by someone else.
I hate Exam Time.

"The Don"
14.06.2020

Nature
(Et amor natura)

Nature is such a wonderous thing.
It's so full of magic & splendour.
It's so full of mystery.
It's so full of imaginings.
It's so full music & songs.
I Love Nature.

Nature is such a wonderful thing.
Nature is so enigmatic & mysterious.
Nature provides us with everything.
Nature gave us birth.
Nature is our home.
I Love Nature.

We are part of Nature.
We are one & the same.
We are part of its beauty.
We are part of its complex web.
We are part of its "Grand Design".
I Love Nature.

Whatever we discover is in Nature.
Whatever we invent is in Nature.
Whatever we desire is in Nature.
Whatever we require is in Nature.
Whatever we need is in Nature.
I Love Nature.

Nature provides us with food.
Nature provides us with shelter.
Nature provides us medicines.
Nature provides us with pleasure.
Nature provides us with air.
I Love Nature.

Nature is everywhere.
Nature is everything.
Nature is the Cosmos.
Nature is unimaginable.
Nature is you & me.
I Love Nature.

We are slowing discovering is many secrets.
It's enormous reservoir of knowledge.
It's database of information.
It doesn't offer them up easily though.
But it's all there for anyone to see.
I Love Nature.

Ah, but there is the conundrum.
That is the riddle you see.
One must see without using your eyes.
That's the key of the mystery.
One must open one's eyes, that's a start.
But one must open one's Heart to see everything.
I Love Nature.

"The Don"
14.06.2020

The Face in the Mirror

I looked at my face in the mirror & what did I see?
The face staring back at me, it wasn't me.
Who was this stranger looking at me?
Because as sure as Hell, the wasn't me.
The face in the mirror, it wasn't me!

Who was this face, that didn't belong to me?
I'd never seen him before & it sure as Hell wasn't me.
The face didn't look a bit like me.
Who was that unknown face staring back at me?
This face in the mirror I do not recognise.

This not me!
I don't like that!
I look like George Clooney.
At least that's what I've been told.
The face in the mirror doesn't look at all like him.

I don't see myself at all.
I'm much more handsome than that.
I'm much younger too, for sure.
This is not me at all.
The face in the mirror is an imposter!

Maybe, I'm the imposter here?
Maybe, it's all been an illusion?
Maybe, it's a complete fabrication?
Maybe, it's my mind playing tricks on me?
Maybe, the face in the mirror IS me?

Oh no, how can that be?
This can't be true?
If what I see is reality?
Then, what is in my mind must be an illusion.
It's a fantasy!
The face in the mirror is the REAL me!

"The Don"
14.06.2020

Feng Shui

There is energy all around.
There are magnetic lines of force surrounding us.
We live inside enormous magnetic fields.
The Earth is one giant magnet.
We are shrouded by electromagnetic radiation.
We exist in an EM ocean.

We have energy pulsating throughout our entire body.
We have magnetic fields penetrating & traveling straight through us.
We are but pawns in this EM ocean.
We are but corks floating upon these EM waves.
Caught in the rip of this great cosmic sea.

One can learn to surf this great ocean.
To become a surfer in this sea.
To catch a wave & ride it.
To tame this great energy.
To conquer these mysterious forces.
To become one with these cosmic energies.

One must allow the energy to flow freely.
There should be no blockages to its path.
No obstacles or impediments to divert its flow.
To allow it to flow freely within you.
This is Feng Shui!
Are you in Feng Shui?

This task is difficult to do.
This is difficult to achieve.
To allow these mighty forces to flow freely.
Flow freely within thee.
But this is one's task.
If you have the mind to do it, to be in Feng Shui.

It requires a lot of discipline.
A lot of power of the mind.
To allow oneself to be completely open.
To remove all resistances from its path
To allow this energy to flow freely within you.
Then, there is Feng Shui.

Are you in Feng Shui?
you oughta be.
Everyone should be!
Feng Shui is the way to be.
Feng Shui is the flow of energy.
Let the energy flow freely, with Feng Shui.

"The Don"
14.06.2020

Synchronicity

(Unus Mundus)

Everything is frequency.
Everything is energy.
Everything is purity.
Everything is fluency.
Everything is fluidity.
Everything is transparency.
Everything is empty.
Everything is moving freely.
Everything is qualitatively.
Everything is spirituality.
Everything is consciously.
Everything is cosmically.
Everything is universally.
Everything is meaningfully.
Everything is metaphysically.
Everything is religiousity.
Everything is unity.
Everything is harmony.
Everything is rhythmically.
Everything is beauty.
Everything is a-causuality.
Everything is simultaneously.
Everything is deeply.
Everything is intentionality.
Everything is inter-dimensionality.
Everything is multiplicity.
Everything is Synchronicity.

"The Don"
15.06.2020

Fascism

(Fascista)

Not having a choice is Fascism.
Being controlled is Fascism.
Being told what to do is Fascism.
Not being allowed to have options is Fascism.
Not being given alternatives is Fascism.
Not being allowed to protest is Fascism.
Not being allowed to object is Fascism.
Not having an opposition is Fascism.
Not being allowed to have alternative points of view is Fascism.
Telling people what to do is Fascism.
Saying, "this is the ONLY way", is Fascism.
Stating that, "this is the way things SHOULD be", is Fascism.

Nazism is Fascism.
Communism is Fascism.
Patriarchy is Fascism.
Totalitarianism is Fascism.
An Oligarchy is Fascism.
A Monarchy is Fascism.
A Dictatorship is Fascism.
A religious state is Fascism.
A military state is Fascism.
A police state is Fascism.

I am Fascism.
You are Fascism.
Racism is Fascism.
God is Fascism.
Society is Fascism.
The whole world is Fascism.

Fascism is FUCKED!

"The Don"
15.06.2020

Road to Nowhere

Where are you going?
What is your final destination?
Where is your journey taking you?
Do you know how it ends?
Do to know what road you're on?
You're on the road to Nowhere.

How long have you been travelling?
Are you tired yet?
Do you know how long you've got to go?
Do you know when you'll get there?
Will you know when you get there?
Because you're on the road to Nowhere.

Have you been travelling long?
Have you come a long way?
Have made many friends?
Have you had places to stay?
Do you know what this highway's called?
'Cause you're on the road to Nowhere.

This is not "Highway 61".
This is not "Route 66".
This is not "Country Roads".
This is not "Roadhouse Blues".
This is not "Highway Star".
This is not "Highway to Hell".
This is not "The Long & Winding Road".
This is not "Thunder Road".
This is not "The Yellow Brick Road".
This is not "Copperhead Road".
This is not "The Bright Side of the Road".
This is not "Tobacco Road".
This is not "Hit the Road Jack".
This is not "Telegraph Road".
This is not "Down the Road A'piece".
This is not "King of the Road".
This the road to Nowhere.

Nowhere is where you've been.
Nowhere is where you're going.
Nowhere is your final destination.
Nowhere is your End.
Nowhere is your Fate.
Nowhere is your final resting place.
Nowhere is the road that you're on.

It doesn't matter which road you take.
Whether it's the high road or the low road.
The back roads or the side streets.
The dirt track or the autostrada.
The long straight road or the bending country roads.
The freeways, motorways or the tollways.
The scenic road or the dusty road.
You're always on the same road.
You're on the road to Nowhere.

"We're on a road to nowhere.
Come on inside.
Taking that ride to nowhere.
We'll take that ride.
I'm feeling okay this morning.
And you know.
We're on the road to paradise.
Here we go, here we go.
…… Would you like to come along?
You can help me sing the song."

We're on a road to nowhere.
But were gonna have some fun.
Come on let's ride.
We're not in any hurry.
We have no deadline to meet.
Because we're on a road to nowhere.
(with thanks to "The Talking Heads").

"The Don"
15.06.2020

You've Gotta Serve Somebody

You think you are your own person?
You think you chart your own course?
You think you can walk your own path?
You think you can run your own race?
Well, think again because you've gotta serve somebody.

You think that you can decide your own destiny?
You think you can do whatever you like?
You think that you live in a Democracy?
You think that you are free?
Well, you are wrong, because you've gotta serve somebody.

It could be the boss man.
It could be the tax man.
It could be mother.
It could be your father.
But you've gotta serve somebody.

It could you brother.
It could be your wife.
It could be your love.
Hell, it could even be your daughter.
But you've gotta serve somebody.

It could be your son.
It could the government.
It could be God.
Hell, it could even be the Devil.
Whomever it is, you've gotta serve somebody.

You could be a servant to your work.
You could be a servant to money.
You could be a servant to fame & fortune.
You could be a to pleasure or pain.
But you've gotta serve somebody.

You could be a servant to vanity.
You could a servant to pride.
You could be a servant to material possessions.
You could be a servant of the Dark Forces.
Whomever it is, you've gotta serve somebody.

"The Don"
15.06.2020

Rich Man, Poor Man

(Are you a wealthy man?)

Are you a rich man?
Are you a poor man?
Are you a troubled man?
Are you a fearful man?
Are you a fearless man?
Are you an honest man?
Are you a dishonest man?
Are you a moral man?
Are you a principled man?
Are you a truthful man?
Are you a good man?
Are you a peaceful man?
Are you a violent man?
Are you a lying man?
Are you an abusive man?
Are you a tolerant man?
Are you a loving man?
Are you a spiritual man?
Are you a religious man?
Are you a wealthy man?

"The Don"
15.06.2020

No Justice

Nessuna Giustizia

You want justice?
You want equity?
You want fairness?
You want equality?
You want respect?
You want to justness?
Well, don't hold your breath.
There is no Justice for you & me.
Because there is no Justice in our society.

There is no Justice if you're poor.
There is no just if you're a woman.
There is no Justice if your "gay".
There is no Justice if you're black.
There is my just if you've been abused.
There is no just if you've been raped.
There is no just if you've been murdered.
There is no Justice for you & me.
Because there is no Justice in our society.

There is justice if you're rich.
There is justice if you've got Power.
There is justice if you're rich & white.
There is justice if you a have rich family.
There is justice if you have a Harvard degree.
There is justice if you are from the aristocracy.
There is justice if you come from the Monarchy.
There is no Justice for you & me.
There is no Justice in our society.

Justice should be equal for everyone.
No matter what colour of your skin.
No matter what gender.
No matter what sexual orientation.
No matter if you are rich or poor.
No matter what station in society you come from.
There is no Justice for you & me.
There is no Justice in our society.

"The Don"
16.06.2020

Do Not Let Worlds Collide

Create many worlds.
Create many lives.
Create many personalities.
Create many stories.
Create many myths.
Create many avatars.
Create many Emojis.
Create many identities.
Create many personas.
But do not let Worlds collide.

Why just have one?
Why not have more?
Why not create as many as you like?
Why not play around?
Why not have some fun?
What not play around with different personalities?
Why not play around with different personas?
Why not be an actor?
Why not let the World be your stage?
But do not let Worlds collide.

It was Will Shakespeare that put it well:
"All the world's a stage,
And all the men and women merely players.
They have their exits and their entrances,
And one man in his time plays many parts,
His acts being seven ages."

So, create many lives.
Create many stages.
Create the best plays that have ever been performed.
Create your masterpiece.
Create your greatest performance!
Create you great character.
But do not let Worlds collide.

"The Don"
16.06.2020

Outraged

Are you outraged?
Well you should be.
There are injustices everywhere.
Police brutality is running rampant.
Black men are be beaten & killed by white male cops.
What the Hell is going on?

Are you outraged?
Well you should be.
Aboriginal juveniles are being bashed & detained for no reason.
White male cops are being excused by saying "they were just having a bad day".
This is not a good state of affairs.

Are you outraged?
Well you should be.
Protesters are told they cannot march on the streets.
Politicians are passing laws making it illegal to protest in public.
"If you do, you'll be breaking the law & you'll be fined or even sent to jail".
That's what they threatened.
This seems like a "Fascist State" to me.

Are you outraged?
Well you should be.
There are statues to our glorious heroes from history.
Until they are found to be slave traders, racists, white supremacists & colonialists.
But we are told we cannot protest because they are our history!
Well, I don't see any statues of Adolf Hitler in Germany!
There is something rotten in our society.

Are you outraged?
Well you should be.
The police a given greater powers to arrest & detain.
Ordinary citizens are having their freedoms taken away, bit by bit.
This is not a good situation.
This is not a good society to be living in.
I fear for our future liberties & freedoms.

Are you outraged?
Well you should be!

"The Don"
16.06.2020

Fear
(Paura)

Fear immobilises.
Fear paralyses.
Fear makes you sweat.
Fear turns you cold.
Fear makes your heart stop.
Fear makes you crazy.
Fear turns you insane.
Do not live in FEAR!

Fear makes you do strange things.
Fear can take over.
Fear can tell you what to do.
Fear can become your master.
Fear makes you tremble.
Fear makes you weak.
Fear makes you meek.
Do not live in FEAR!

Fear can control your life.
Fear can take over.
Fear can dominate.
Fear shows no mercy.
Fear turns you catatonic.
Fear is a Destroyer.
Fear ruins your life.
Do not live in FEAR!

Fear makes you cautious.
Fear makes you timid.
Fear makes you scared.
Fear makes you panic.
Fear gives you cold sweats at night.
Fear doesn't let you sleep at night.
Fear gives you nightmares, awake or asleep.
Do not live in FEAR!

Fear stops you from taking risks.
Fear stops you from taking challenges.
Fear stops you from trying new things.
Fear stops you from having adventures.
Fear stops you from being creative.
Fear stops you from becoming a better person.
Fear stops you from loving deeply & honestly.
Do not live in FEAR!

Fear kills your passion.
Fear kills your desire.
Fear kills your vitality.
Fear kills your libido.
Fear kills your imagination.
Fear kills your "joie de vivre".
Fear kills your want to live.
Fear kills your integrity.
Fear kills your morality.
Fear kills your principles.
Fear kills your heart.
Fear kills your soul.
Fear kills your very Being.
Fear kills!

Do not live in FEAR!

"The Don"
17.06.2020

Let's fuck!

(Scopiamo!)

Let's make Lo♥e.
Let's have sex.
Let's bonk.
Let's root.
Let's bang.
Let's screw.
Let's mate.
Let's Coitus.
Let's shag.
Let's conjugate.
Let's fool about.
Let's play around.
Let's bond.
Let's fornicate.
Let's copulate.
Let's consummate.
Let's get it on.
Let's lay.
Let's ride.
Let's merge.
Let's hook up.
Let's mount.
Let's hitch.
Let's conjoin.
Let's entwine.
Let's interlock.
Let's dalliance.

Let's roll in the hay.
Let's come together.
Let's go to bed.
Let's Rock'n'Roll.

Let's have intercourse.
Let's have a union.
Let's have intimate relations.
Let's have some penetration.
Let's have sexual intercourse.
Let's have some nookie.
Let's have some rumpy pumpy.
Let's have carnal knowledge.
Let's have some hanky panky.
Let's have some horizontal hula.
Let's have some monkey business.
Let's have some Morning Glory.
Let's have some Afternoon Delight.
Let's have a Midnight Snack.

Let's make whoopee!
Let's make birds & the bees.
Let's make some sweet romance.

Let's fuck!

"The Don"
17.06.2020

Orgasm Addict

I like pleasure.
I like pain.
I like sex.
I like masturbating.
I like to cum.
I'm an orgasm addict.

I like desire.
I like fun.
I like women.
I like pussy.
I like bums.
I'm an orgasm addict.

I like nudity.
I like the naked female body.
I like titties.
I like lips.
I like toes.
I'm an orgasm addict.

I like tonguing.
I like licking.
I like biting.
I like sucking.
I like fucking.
I'm an orgasm addict.

I like poking.
I like fingering.
I like petting.
I like eating.
I like penetrating.
I'm an orgasm addict.

I like to arouse.
I like to be aroused.
I like to be erotic.
I like to be eroticised.
I like to be fucked.
I'm an orgasm addict.

I like to explode with passion.
I like to explode with desire.
I like to be consumed by ecstasy.
I like to be enveloped by your sexual appetite.
I like to be swallowed by your fire.
I'm an orgasm addict.

"The Don"
17.06.2020

The Dance of Life
(La danza della vita)

First there is the sperm & the egg.
Together they copulate & fuse as one.
Fertilisation has occurred.
The first cell of you has been created.
The Dance of Life has begun.

The first cell explodes with exponential growth.
1, 2, 4, 8, 32, 64, 128, 256, 512, 1024...
In a matter of seconds this takes place.
Nature is truly an amazing thing.
The Dance of Life has started.

This is the embryo.
Just a blob of cells.
Furiously & feverishly reproducing.
Each cell perfectly identical to the other.
The Dance of Life is gathering pace.

The dance is well coordinated.
The instructions codified in your DNA.
Step 1, step 2, step 3, step 4 & on & on.
It never slips a step.
The Dance of Life has an excellent flow.

By week 8 or there abouts, the fetus takes form.
A heart will begin to beat.
Differentiated organs begin to appear.
Like hands, fingers, eyes, ears, mouth, legs & feet.
The Dance of Life is has become expressive.

The womb is not a quiet place.
There are sounds from all over the place.
But the loudest sound for sure.
Is the beat of your mother's heart.
The Dance of Life is moving to the rhythm of the beat.

The womb,
Your first home,
Your sanctuary.
Your secret place.
The Dance of Life's first dance floor.

The womb is a safe place.
A place that you call home.
But by month number 9 you will be ejected.
Into the cruel you will unwilling enter crying.
The Dance of Life has started to Rock'n'Roll.

"The Don"
18.06.2020

The Dance of Death

(La danza della morte)
(Dance Macabre)

It's just a blink of an eye.
It's just a click of your fingers.
It's just a heartbeat away.
It's just a nano second away.
The dance of death is your last dance.

The last dance can be a slow waltz.
It might be a passionate, fiery Tango.
It could be the vivacious Macarena or the Samba.
Generally though, you have no choice in the matter.
The dance of death will last forever.

You won't see it coming.
You won't here it's footsteps.
It doesn't send a warning.
It likes to surprise & scare.
The dance of death starts without your consent.

It taps you on the shoulder.
"Can I have the next dance?", it asks.
You cannot refuse.
As you look into its eyes.
The dance of death has started whether you like or not.

It's not as bad you were led to believe.
It's not as bad as you imagined.
Death is actually quite a good dancer.
Given how long the dance has existed
The dance of death has own identity.

Death will hold you close.
It will hug you & let you sway.
It will whisper sweet words into your ears.
It will kiss you on your lips.
The dance of death tastes so sweet.

Death will touch your brow.
Put you mind to rest.
Close your eyelids with two kisses.
But it's hand upon your heart & make it go to sleep.
The dance of death has finished & now you are Dead.

"The Don"
28.06.2020

A Cry in the Wind

Sharon, why don't you call?
Yanet, why don't you call?
"Juicy Julie", why don't you call?
Su, why don't you call?
Sheila, why don't you call?
Vanessa, why don't you call?
Beccy, why don't you call?
Ren, why don't you call?
Livvy, why don't you call?
Vita, why don't you call?
Daniele, why don't you call?
Sarah, why don't you call?
Antonia, why don't you call?
Lucia, why don't you call?
Nada, why don't you call?
Susan, why don't you call?
Jady, why don't you call?
Yuriko, why don't you call?
Feten, why don't you call?
Jennifer, why don't you call?
Jessie, why don't you call?
Scarlett, why don't you call?
Isabel, why don't you call?
Kirstie, why don't you call?
Yenifer, why don't you call?
Anna, why don't you call?
Ella, why don't you call?
Max, why don't you call?
SaraMae Belle, why don't you call?
Maddie, why don't you call?
Rose, why don't you call?

I Lo♥e you, one & all.
To all of you, why don't you call?
I'm here waiting by the phone.
Waiting, waiting for you call.
But no one calls.
The phone is dead.
I'm waiting, waiting for your call.

It you ever think about me sometime.
If I ever cross your mind.
If I ever enter your head.
Just for a fleeting moment.
Give me a call.
My number is still the same.
1800Lo♥e, that's how you'll get me.
I'm always here, why don't you call?

It's just a cry in the wind.
A feather in the breeze.
Maybe it flies high into the skies
Maybe it will find you wherever you are.
It's just a thought, just a passing desire.
It's just a cry in the wind.

"The Don"
18.06.2020

Let's Get High!

Let's do drugs.
Let's do smoke some dope.
Let's snort so cocaine.
Let's drop some ACID.
Let's get HIGH.

Let's smoke some "Hooch".
Let's do some Ecstasy.
Let's drop some LSD.
Let's do some MDMA.
Let's get HIGH.

Let's get stoned.
Let's get out of it.
Let's get blown away.
Let's get spaced out.
Let's get HIGH.

Let's eat some "Marijuana Cookies"
Let's smoke "Grass".
Let's smoke some "Hashish".
Let's do some psychotropic drugs.
Let's get HIGH.

Let's have some "Mary Jane".
Let's smoke some "Hash Oil".
Let's smoke some "Gunja".
Let's some "NO".
Let's get HIGH.

Let's eat some "Magic Mushrooms".
Let's smoke some "Peyote".
Let's take some "Meth".
Let's drop some hallucinations.
Let's get HIGH.

Let's blow our minds.
Let's blow our brains.
Let's blow some cones.
Let's blow some joints.
Let's get HIGH.

Let's touch the sky.
Let's touch the heavens.
Let's touch our inner selves.
Let's touch our very souls.
Let's get HIGH.

Let's never come back down.
Let's never get back on the ground.
Let's never come back to this cruel world.
Let's never leave this "Happy Place".
Let's get HIGH.

Let's stay forever in this idyllic place.
Let's stay forever in this peaceful space.
Let's stay forever in this cosmic realm.
Let's stay forever in wonderment & fantasy.
Let's get HIGH forever!

"The Don"
18.06.2020

Perversion

(Perversione)

Perversity.
Deviancy.
Unnatural.
Depravity.
Abnormality.
Deviant.
Aberrant.
Deranged.
Kinky.
Debauchery.
Vice.
Wickedness.
Degeneracy.
Immorality.
Deviance.
Aberration.
Distorted.
Abnormal.
Deviation.
Pervert.
Disgusting.
Abhorrent.
Distortion.
Satanic.
Devilish.
Lucifer.
Beelzebub.
Scaramouche.

Subversion.
Conversion.
Dispersion.
Conversion.
Submersion.
Diversion.
Immersion.
Reversion.
Aversion.
Interspersion.
Version.
Inversion.
Reconversion.
Ambiversion.
Emersion.
Introversion.
Extroversion.
Bioconversion.
Obversion.

Confusion.
Contusion.
Illusion.
Protrusion.
Inclusion.
Diffusion.
Transfusion.
Fusion.
Disillusion.
Conclusion.
Delusion.
disillusion.
transfusion.

"The Don"
19.02.2020

Forbidden Fruits

Don't touch me there.
Don't keep the lights on.
Don't swear.
Don't be naked.
Don't say f**k.
Don't be kinky.
Don't like naked girls.
Forbidden fruits are always more delicious.

Don't play with yourself.
Don't enjoy your sexuality.
Don't enjoy carnal pleasures.
Don't get high.
Don't enjoy pleasuring yourself.
Don't enjoy your orgasm.
Don't enjoy sex.
Forbidden fruits always taste more delicious.

Don't masturbate.
Don't fornicate.
Don't commit adultery.
Don't fool around with someone else's wife.
Don't seek pleasures of the flesh.
Don't lick pussy.
Don't eat a juicy fig out one.
Forbidden fruits are always more delicious.

Don't ever smother a naked body with cream & strawberries.
Don't ever pour chocolate topping on one's titties.
Don't put honey in the honey pot
Don't lick it all off.
Don't put brandy custard in the muff pie.
Don't lick & suck it dry.
Don't think about rolling together & having a good time.
Don't be sinful, it's not God's way.
Forbidden fruits always taste more delicious.

Forbidden fruits are what we all dream about.
Forbidden fruits are what get us excited.
Forbidden fruits are what make us sweaty.
Forbidden fruits are what leave us breathless.
Forbidden fruits are what make us wet.
Forbidden fruits are what we live for.
Forbidden fruits are what we are told not to have.
Forbidden fruits are always more delicious exactly because they are FORBIDDEN!

Forbidden Fruits

"The Don",
19.06.2030

Flatulation

(The farting Game)

It's all about gases.
It's called Methane.
It's a natural process.
So, don't keep it in.
Let all out.
Don't mess about.
Let your 'bum trumpet" sing.
Let it play a tune.
The louder the better.

You can fart in public.
Just walk & fart.
Fart with confidence.
Fart with style.
So, "fart away!", I say.

Nobody likes a "SbD".
Although it's a lot of fun.
To blame someone.
That's standing close to you.
So, no one thinks it's you.
That let off such a STINKER.
"Did you just let one off?"
Is what you have to say.
So that doubt is cast away.
"It wasn't me!".
You'll hear them say.
Too late!
The damage has been done.
The cat is out of the bag.
The spotlight is on them.
They are wounded.
Now, to really tie it up.
"OMG, it was you!
How disgusting!"
The game is over.
You have won.
Everyone moves away.

Stunned by what has just happened.
They stand alone.
Innocence does not matter.
When it comes to the bum.

If this ever happens to you.
Remember there is only one thing you must do.
Take it like a man.
Bare & grin.
For a fart is a powerful force.
And one you cannot defeat.

But bide your time.
For revenge is sweet.
Make sure to get in first.
The next you meet.
Let one off.
Let the game commence.
This is a good test for you.
To see if you can get your so deserved REVENGE.
But the pressure is on you.
To choose the right moment.
To get it just right.
Because a "Silent but Deadly",
Is not easy to do well.
It takes years of practice.
To fart without a noise.

But this is the art.
It's all in the technique.
To let it flow freely.
Without too much force.
Otherwise there will be a sound.
And then the game is up.
For you will have given yourself away.
And there is nothing you can say.
There is nothing you can do.
But take the blame.
Because you have just lost.
The farting game.

Whatever you do.
Don't do a sloppy & wet.
Because that's the quick end.
To the farting game.

"The Don"
20.06.202

Lo♥e Yourself

Believe in yourself.
Have faith in yourself.
Be kind to yourself.
Treat yourself well.
Be your best friend.
Lo♥e yourself.

Never put yourself down.
Never doubt youself.
Never abuse yourself.
Never put yourself into the ground.
Never hate yourself.
Lo♥e yourself.

Always treat yourself well.
Always be kind to yourself.
Always forgive yourself.
Always trust yourself.
Always be your best friend.
Always Lo♥e yourself.

Tell yourself that you are the best.
Tell yourself that you are okay.
Tell yourself that you don't need to worry.
Tell yourself that everything will work out.
Tell yourself that you are the one.
Tell yourself to always Lo♥e yourself.

You are unique.
You are the only one.
There is nobody else the world like you.
There is nobody else the whole COSMOS like you.
You are YOU & that is that.
So, Lo♥e Yourself, because that's ALL you've got!

Me, myself & I.
That's there is.
The Triad of identity.
The Triad of Power.
The Triad of who I am.
Lo♥e Yourself, because you are 3 in 1.

"The Don"
20.06.2020

If You're Gonna Smell, Smell Beautiful

If you're staying at home, smell beautiful.
If you're going out, smell beautiful.
If gonna have a good time, smell beautiful.
If you going on a date, smell beautiful.
If you're gonna stay out late, smell beautiful.
If you're gonna make out, smell beautiful.
If you're gonna make Lo e, smell beautiful.
If you're gonna stay overnight, smell beautiful.
If you're gonna go cruisin', smell beautiful.
If you're gonna smell, smell beautiful.

If looking for some oozing, smell beautiful.
If you're looking for fun, smell beautiful.
If you're looking for a good time, smell beautiful.
If you're looking for some Lo in', smell beautiful.
If you're looking for some action, smell beautiful.
If you're looking for playtime, smell beautiful.
If you're looking for a good night, smell beautiful.
If you're looking for someone to make you feel right, smell beautiful.
If you're looking to get high, smell beautiful.
If you're gonna smell, smell beautiful.

"The Don"
20.06.2020

I Like it Rough

So, you think that you're tough.
You think that you're Harley Quinn.
You've got tattoos.
You like the Blues.
You like to think that you live on the streets.
You say, "I like it rough!"

You like to play dirty.
You like to be in control.
You like a bit of power.
But don't let it go to your soul.
Don't fool yourself.
Just because you say, "I like it rough!"

You better watch out.
You better take care.
'Cause when you put yourself out there.
Nobody cares.
It's a mean ol' world, that's for sure.
So, you'd better be careful when you say, "I like it rough!"

Who's got your back?
Do you have a "plan"?
Do you have an exit strategy?
Do know where turn?
Them's the risks you take.
When you fly solo & say, "I like it rough!"

What will you do, when you are exposed?
What will you do, when your mask is ripped off?
What will you do, when your "real" identity is revealed?
What will you do, when everyone sees who you really are?
Be careful you're not a fake when you say, "I like it rough!".

It's a dangerous game that you're playing.
It's a tough world that we're living in.
You need to be tough to survive out there.
Otherwise, you'll be eaten alive.
So, I understand why you are doing it.
So, remember, I'll be there if you need someone, when you say, "I like it rough!".

'The Don"
20.06.2020

A Good Life!
(Buona Vita)

When the Fat Lady sings.
When the bell tolls for thee.
When the curtain comes down.
When the lights go out.
When your song has been sung.
When it's all said & done.
Make sure you've had a good life!

When the race had been run.
When you've crossed the finishing line.
When the ref. has blown his whistle.
When the game is all over.
When you've kicked you're last goal.
When you've taken your last breath.
Make sure you've had a good life!

When you had your last meal.
When you've drunk your last beer.
When you've outlasted your stay.
When you've been kicked out the door.
When you've collapsed on the floor
When you've had your last hoorah.
Make sure you've had a good life!

When you've painted your masterpiece.
When you've written your memoirs.
When your story's been told.
When your jokes have run out.
When your pockets are empty.
When you've got no more fuel in the tank.
Make sure you've had a good life!

When you've had your last kiss.
When you've touched your last flesh.
When you've stroked your last pussy.
When you've had last lay.
When you've come for the last time.
When you lay down to rest.
Make sure you've had a good life!

"The Don"
20.06.2020

Murder Most Foul

There's been a murder in your street.
There's been a killing at your feet.
There is a killer on the loose.
There's a prowler in our road.
There is injustice in the air.
Some a claiming it was the police.
That carried out this heinous crime.
This murder most foul.

The man was innocent.
He was just out walking his dog.
He didn't see it coming.
He was hit from behind.
It was a cowardly act.
His head hit the ground.
It cracked open like a coconut.
There was blood & brain matter everywhere.
It was definitely a murder most foul.

"It was a case of mistaken identity".
That's what was claimed.
George Floyd was his name.
He was black.
I guess that says it all.
He was in the wrong place at the wrong time.
That's how it goes with a murder most foul.

The police said he was armed.
But no weapon was ever found.
They say they thought he was the one.
That they were looking for.
"It was dark.
It happened so quickly.
He tried to run away", they said.
But nevertheless, it was a murder most foul.

"What was he doing walking around late at night?
He should be in bed with his wife.
Safe & sound tucked away in his home.
Not walking the dark streets alone.
He was asking for trouble being outside.
He must've been looking for trouble.
Because that's what he found with a murder most foul".

People gather around the spot where he died.
There a flowers & tributes about how they're sorry at the loss of his life.
But that won't bring him back.
That won't be enough.
What's gonna happen to his children & his wife?
Will there be justice for this man?
Who died a lonely death?
His skull cracked open.
Will those that carried out this crime ever be punished?
And be made to pay for a murder most foul.

"The Don"
20.06.2020

Lost Innocence

(L'innocence Perdue)

When I was a little boy back then.
Such a long time ago.
I remember these fantastic theme songs.
From classic television shows of the 1960s.
They are still playing in my head now.
Even though it's been 5 score years plus 10.
It's like no time has passed at all.
They didn't write them like that anymore.

"Top Cat"
About "Top Cat" leader of a cool, crazy group of cats.

"Top Cat!
The most effectual!
Top Cat!
Who's intellectual!
Close friends get to call him "T.C.,"
Providing it's with dignity!

Top Cat!
The indisputable leader of the gang.
He's the boss, he's a VIP, he's a championship.
He's the most tip top,
Top Cat.

Yes, he's the chief, he's a king,
But above everything,
He's the most tip top,
Top Cat!

Top Cat!"

"Prince Planet"
About an alien boy sent here from planet "Radon" to save Earth.

"Here comes Prince Planet!
Priiiiince Planet!"

"Gigantor"
About the world's mightiest robot controlled by "Jimmy Spark" that saves lives.

"Gigantor, Gigantor, Gigantor.

Gigantor the space aged robot,
He is at your command.
Gigantor the space aged robot,
His power is in your hand.

Bigger than big, taller than tall,
Quicker than quick, stronger than strong.
Ready to fight for right, against wrong.

Gigantor, Gigantor, Gigantor."

Songwriters: Bob Harris/Paul Francis Webster

"Marine Boy"
About a teenage boy who lives under water & battles evil to keep the oceans safe.

"He is a boy, a very special boy.
Powered by propeller shoes, flying Sub ahoy! Whooshing through the water on a friendly dolphin's back.

Racing to the rescue of victims of attack.
In a flash, he'll foil the foe,

With a quick boomerang throw!
Loyal friend of the sea to the end.

Is our Marine Boy"

"The Monkeys"
Follows the madcap & hilarious adventures of four young, zany boys trying to make a name for themselves as a rock 'n roll band in the 1960s.

"The Monkees"

"Here we come.
Walkin' down the street.
We get the funniest looks from.
Everyone we meet.

Hey, hey, we're the Monkees.
And people say we monkey around.
But we're too busy singing.
To put anybody down.

We go wherever we want to.
Do what we like to do.
We don't have time to get restless.
There's always something new.

Hey, hey, we're the Monkees.
And people say we monkey around.
But we're too busy singing.
To put anybody down.

We're just tryin' to be friendly.
Come and watch us sing and play.
We're the young generation.
And we've got something to say, oh.

Any time.
Or anywhere.
Just look over your shoulder.
Guess who'll be standing there?

Hey, hey, we're the Monkees.
And people say we monkey around.
But we're too busy singing.
To put anybody down.

Whaaa, one time!

Hey, hey, we're the Monkees
And people say we monkey around.
But we're too busy singing.
To put anybody down.
We're just tryin' to be friendly.
Come and watch us sing and play.
We're the young generation.
And we've got something to say.

Hey, hey, we're the Monkees.
Hey, hey, we're the Monkees."

Songwriters: Bobby Hart/Tommy Boyce

"Daniel Boone"

Daniel Boone was a frontiers man in the 1880s of America. He wore a "coonskin cap" & had "Mingo", an American Cherokee Indian, as his sidekick.

"The Ballad of Daniel Boone"

"Daniel Boone was a man. Yes, a big man.
With an eye like an eagle and as tall as a mountain was he.
Daniel Boone was a man. Yes, a big man.
He was brave, he was fearless and as tough as a mighty oak tree.

From the coonskin cap on the top of ol' Dan to the heel of his rawhide shoe
The rippin'est roarin'est fightin'est man the frontier ever knew.

Daniel Boone was a man. Yes, a big man.

What a Boone. What a dooer. What a dream come a truer was he."

Songwriters: Vera Matson/Lionel Newman

"Magila Gorilla"

About a goofy, talking gorilla that is try to be sold by "Mr Peeples".

"Gorilla
Magila Gorilla for sale!
(How much is that Gorilla in the window?)

Take our advice
At any price
A gorilla like Magila is mighty nice!
Gorilla

Magila Gorilla for sale!"

Songwriter: Hoyt Curtin

"Astro Boy"

About an android boy with human emotions.

"There you go Astroboy.
On your flight into space.
Rocket high.
Through the sky.
More adventures to do all day.

Astroboy bombs away.
On your mission today.
There's a countdown.
And a blastoff.
Everyday is go Astroboy.

Astroboy as you fly.
Strange new worlds you will spy.
Atom-celled.
Jet propelled.
Fighting monsters high in the sky.

Astroboy there you go.
Will you fight friend or foe.
Cosmic ranger.
Laugh at danger.
Everyday is go Astroboy.

Astroboy as you fly.
Strange new worlds you will spy.
Atom-celled.
Jet propelled.
Fighting monsters high in the sky.

Astroboy there you go.
Will you fight friend or foe.
Crowds will cheer you.
You're a hero.
As you go, go, go Astroboy."

"Green Acres"

About a New York lawyer & his Hungarian wife whom decide to make 'seachange" from a swanky Manhattan apartment to live on a farm.

"Green acres is the place to be.
Farm livin' is the life for me.
Land spreadin' out so far and wide.
Keep Manhattan, just give me that countryside.

New York is where I'd rather stay.
I get allergic smelling hay.
I just adore a penthouse view.
Dahling I love you but give me Park Avenue.

*The chores, the stores.
Fresh air, Times Square.*

*You are my wife.
Good bye, city life.
Green acres we are there."*

Songwriter: Mizzy Vic

"The Beverley Hillbillys"

About a poor, backwoods family from the hills of the Ozark Mountains, who move to posh Beverly Hills, California after striking oil on their land.

"The Ballad of Jed Clampett"

*Come and listen to a story about a man named Jed.
A poor mountaineer, barely kept his family fed,
Then one day he was shootin' at some food,
And up through the ground came a bubblin crude.*

Oil that is, black gold, Texas tea.

*Well the first thing you know ol' Jed's a millionaire,
Kinfolk said Jed move away from there.
Said Californy is the place you ought to be.
So, they loaded up the truck and moved to Beverly.*

*Hills, that is. Swimmin' pools, movie stars."
"Well now, it's time to say good-bye to Jed and all his kin.
And they would like to thank you folks fer kindly droppin' in.
You're all invited back next week to this locality.
To have a heapin' helpin' of their hospitality*

*Hillbilly that is. Set a spell. Take your shoes off.
Y'all come back now, y'hear?"*

Songwriters: Paul Henning

"Spiderman"

About Peter Parker, a teenage boy that gets bitten by a radioactive spider which gives him spiderlike abilities.

*"Spiderman, Spiderman, does whatever a spider can
Spins a web any size, catches thieves just like flies
Look out, here comes the Spiderman"*

Is he strong? Listen bud, he's got radioactive blood
Can he swing from a thread? Take a look overhead
Hey, there! There goes the Spiderman

In the chill of the night, At the scene of a crime
Like a streak of light, he arrives just in time

Spiderman, Spiderman, friendly neighbourhood, Spiderman
Wealth and fame, he ignores, action is his reward
Look out, here comes the Spiderman

Spiderman, Spiderman, friendly neighbourhood, Spiderman
Wealth and fame, he ignores, action is his reward
To him, life's a great big bang up, whenever there's a hang up,
You'll find the Spiderman!"

Songwriters: Paul Francis Webster / J. Robert Harris

"Happy Days"

Who can forget "The Fonz" & the gang.
What a wonderful show of lost innocence.
Yes, they were indeed, "Happy Days"!

"Happy Days
Sunday, Monday, Happy Days,
Tuesday, Wednesday, Happy Days,
Thursday, Friday, Happy Days,
Saturday, what a day,
Rockin all week with you.
This day is ours
Won't you be mine. (Oh Happy Days)
This day is ours (Oh Happy Days)."

Songwriters: Derek Allen/Bobby Brown

"Gilligan's Island"

About a group of 7 tourists that go on a 7 hour trip & get shipwrecked & stranded on a uncharted island.

"Just sit right back and you'll hear a tale, a tale of a fateful trip.
That started from this tropic port, aboard this tiny ship.
The mate was a mighty sailing man, the skipper brave and sure.
Five passengers set sail that day, on a three-hour tour.
A three-hour tour.

The weather started getting rough, the tiny ship was tossed.
If not for the courage of the fearless crew the Minnow would be lost.
The Minnow would be lost.

The Minnow would be lost.

*The ship set ground on the shore of this uncharted desert isle.
With Gilligan, the Skipper too.
The millionaire and his wife.
The movie star, Professor and Mary Ann.
Here on Gilligan's Isle.*

*So, this is the tale of our castaways, they're here for a long, long time.
They'll have to make the best of things, and it's an uphill climb.
The first mate and his skipper too will do their very best.
To make the others comfortable, in the tropic island nest.
No phones, no lights, no motor cars, not a single luxury.
Like Robinson Crusoe, it's primitive as can be.
So, join us here each week my friend, you're sure to get a smile.
From seven stranded Castaways, here on Gilligan's Isle.*

*Yeah, it's Gilligan, the Skipper too.
The millionaire and his wife.
The movie star, professor and Mary Ann.
Here on Gilligan's Isle."*

Songwriters: George Wyle / Sherwood Schwartz

These were truly great times to be a child.
There was an innocence.
An innocence that has now been lost.
It was time of *"Flower Power"*.
The time of *"Make Lo ❤ e Not War!"*.
It was the time of *"LSD"*.
It was the time of the *"Counterculture"*.
It was the time of *"wearing flowers in your hair"*.
It was the time of the *"Hippies"*.
It was the time of *"Timothy Leary"*.
It was the time to *"Turn on, Tune in, Drop out"*.
It was the time of *"Free Lo ❤ e"*.
It was the time of *"The Beatles"*.
It was the time of *"The Rolling Stones"*.
It was the time of *"Bob Dylan"*.
It was the time of *"Jimi Hendrix"*.
It was the time of the *"Newport Folk Festival"*.
It was the time of *"Monterey"*.
It was the time of *"Woodstock"*.
It was the time of *"Apollo 11"*

It was the time of *walking on the Moon*.

A time of innocence & wonder.
It's a new world today.
It's a cruel world today.
We have lost our youth.
We have lost our innocence.
A part of me longs for that lost innocence.

I carry it inside me though.
It is like a burning flame.
I will never let that flame die.
Not until the very end.
And even then, who knows?
That flame might still keep burning then?
That flame that might burn forever.
That flame of lost innocence.

"San Francisco"
"If you're going to San Francisco.
Be sure to wear some flowers in your hair.
If you're going to San Francisco.
You're gonna meet some gentle people there.

For those who come to San Francisco.
Summertime will be a love-in there.
In the streets of San Francisco.
Gentle people with flowers in their hair.

All across the nation.
Such a strange vibration.
People in motion.
There's a whole generation.
With a new explanation.
People in motion.
People in motion.

For those who come to San Francisco.
Be sure to wear some flowers in your hair.
If you come to San Francisco.
Summertime will be a love-in there.

If you come to San Francisco.
Summertime will be a love-in there."

Sung by: Scott McKenzie
Songwriter: John Edmund Andrew Phillips

"The Don"
21.06.2020

Death of Innocence
(Mort d'innocence)

They shot JFK in the head.
His brother, Robert Kennedy, was murdered too.
They shot Martin Luther King.
There were riots & 4 deaths at the Altamont Free Concert.
There was the "Cold War".
There was the "Vietnam War".
There were "Napalm bombs".
There was the US Nuclear Testing at Bikini Atoll in the South Pacific.
There was the French Nuclear Testing at Mururoa Atoll also in the South Pacific.
There was the British Nuclear Testing at Maralinga in South Australia.
There was the displacement of Aboriginal peoples from their native lands.
There were lies that no one lived out there claimed by the Australian Government.

There was the death of Jim Morrison.
There was the death of Jimi Hendrix.
There was the death of Janice Joplin.
There was the death of Innocence.

Innocence is the first to die.
Innocence can never be revived.
Innocence once list is lost forever.
Innocence once gone is gone.
Innocence will never return.
Innocence is a *"Paradise Lost"*.
Innocence is the *"Garden of Eden"*.
Innocence is Dead!
The Death of Innocence.

We have lost our Innocence.
Maybe we misplaced it some place.
Will we ever be able to regain it.
Or will it be forever gone?
Will we be able to find it once more?
Do we even want to?
Maybe it's better this way?
Some might say.
To have the Death of Innocence.

Am I delusional?
Was it all a dream?
Maybe it wasn't like that at all?
Maybe it was all "make believe"?
Maybe I'm kidding myself?
Maybe I'm a fool?
Maybe Innocence never really existed?
Maybe it was just in my head?
Maybe there was no Innocence?
Maybe there was no Death of Innocence?
Maybe Innocence didn't exist at all?

Mort d'innocence

"The Don"
21.06.2020

Déjà Vu

It's happened before.
Here we go again.
It's all in the Past.
I've been here before.
Is this a revolving door.
I'm falling to the floor.
It's called *Déjà Vu*.

I know who you are.
Have we met before?
It's happening again.
History's repeating.
I can feel my heart beating.
It's a Space-Time Discontinuim.
I'm in *Déjà Vu*.

It's a strange sensation.
A tingling up & down your spine.
It's sorta creepy & exciting.
It's a bit spooky & frightening.
It can happen at any time.
O Oh, it's happening again.
It's *Déjà Vu*.

Does it ever happen to you?
Is this something new?
Am I going crazy?
I'm going mad?
Am I insane?
Is it all just in my brain?
This thing called *Déjà Vu*?

I think we've met before.
On some distant shore.
In another time & place.
We were making sweet love.
We saw stars up above.
It was a rainy night.
Is this just *Déjà Vu*?

Is this a Spiritual thing?
Is this a sign that there's something more?
Is this a metaphysical door?
To another time & place?
To another Reality?
To another Space?
To a place called *Déjà Vu*.

"The Don"
22.06.2020

Game of Empires

The need to rule.
The desire for power.
The want to control.
The greed for riches.
The thirst for immortality.
Let's play the Game of Empires.

It started from the earliest of times.
There was The Greek Empire.
With its love of the male physical form.
The home of The Olympic Games
The great architecture & art.
We've started playing the Game of Empires.

The Phoenician Empire.
A great trading nation.
The Assyrian Empire.
With the great Hammurabi
The Babylonian Empire.
We're playing the Game of Empires.

The Egyptian Empire.
Was it really an Empire?
It lasted a very long time.
Ruled by many pharaohs.
Who can forget Queen Nefertiti or Cleopatra?
I'm loving playing the Game of Empires.

Then the was the greatest empire of all.
It was the Roman Empire.
It lasted one thousand years.
It gave us Emperors, Caesar, aqueducts, roads & concrete.
Who does not love a "Roman Bath"?
Oh, what fun it is playing the Game of Empires.

Then we move onto The Byzantine Empire.
With its capital at Constantinople.
Its Byzantine art is so beautiful.
A delight to the eyes.
It also gave us it's baths.
I'm naked now whilst playing the Game of Empires.

Then there was the Ming Dynasty in China.
The Mongolian Empire.
The Aztec Empire in South America
The Spanish Empire with its cruel & brutal "Conquistadors".
I'm sweating now, playing the Game of Empires.

The insidious Roman Catholic Church Empire.
Although, strictly speaking not really an Empire.
It spread its tentacles all around the world.
Creating massive horrors in its path.
All in the name of God, what atrocities were committed.
I'm crying now whilst playing the Game of Empires.

With its capital in Vatican City.
Ruled by the Pope.
It polluted the minds of millions of people.
Destroyed thousands of cultures.
And the most terrible thing, it's still doing it today.
I'm angry now playing this Game of Empires.

There was the Ottoman Empire.
The French Empire.
The Prussian Empire.
The Russian Empire.
The German Empire
I'm beginning to hate playing the Game of Empires.

The most expansive empire of all.
With its colonising ways.
Was the British Empire.
It still exists today under a different name.
It is called The British Commonwealth headed by The Queen.
It's very exhausting playing the Game of Empires.

There are still Empires today.
Though they no longer call themselves such.
There is Russia, China & The USA.
The triad of power, the rests in hands.
They rule the world. rests in hands.
Once started, there is no end, to the Game of Empires.

"The Don"
22.06.2020

The 3 Acts of Sex

There are the 10 commandments.
1: Thou shalt have no other gods before me.
2: Honour thy father and thy mother.
3: Remember the sabbath day, to keep it holy.
4: Thou shalt not make unto thee any graven image.
5: Thou shalt not take the name of the Lord thy God in vain.
6: Thou shalt not kill.
7: Thou shalt not commit adultery.
8: Thou shalt not steal.
9: Thou shalt not bear false witness against thy neighbour.
10: Thou shalt not covet.

There are the 7 Deadly Sins.
1: Pride.
2: Greed.
3: Wrath.
4: Envy.
5: Lust.
6: Gluttony.
7: Sloth.

There are the 7 Wonders of the Ancient world.
1: The Great Pyramid of Giza.
2: The Colossus of Rhodes.
3: The Lighthouse of Alexandria.
4: The Mausoleum at Halicarnassus.
5: The Temple of Artemis.
6: The Statue of Zeus.
7: The Hanging Gardens of Babylon

The 7 Wonders of The Natural World.
1: Mount Everest. Mount Everest
2: Harbour of Rio de Janeiro.
3: Great Barrier Reef.
4: Victoria Falls.
5: Paricutin Volcano.
6: The Grand Canyon.
7: The Aurora Borealis.

Then, there are the 3 Acts of Sex.
1: Vaginal sex.
2: Anal sex.
3: Oral sex.
These are the greatest of them all.
For without them life would not be worth living for.

"Vaginal Sex" between a male & a female.
When a cock penetrates a pussy.
"Anal Sex", for those that like a cock up the arse.
"Oral Sex", sucking a cock in your mouth is called *"Fellatio"*.
Licking a pussy with your tongue is called *"Cunnilingus"*.

All are good & they not a sin.
So, why not try them out.
The next time you have the whim.
There easy to do.
No instructions required.
Just let your body do the work.
Your passion be your driver.
The 3 Acts of Desire.
The 3 Acts of Sex.

The 3 Acts of Sex

"The Don"
22.06.2020

Non-Violence

Non-Violence is not gutless.
Non-Violence is not passivity.
Non-Violence is not giving in.
Non-Violence is not being cowardly.
Non-Violence is not giving up.
Non-Violence is not being weak.
Non-Violence is not giving up.
Non-Violence is not allowing violence to win.

Non-Violence is bravery.
Non-Violence is heroic.
Non-Violence is strength.
Non-Violence is power.
Non-Violence is principled.
Non-Violence is dignity.
Non-Violence is moral.
Non-Violence is beautiful.
Non-Violence is Lo♥e.

Non-Violence is all about resistance.
Non-Violence is all about action.
Non-Violence is all about creating a vacuum.
Non-Violence is all about rebellion.
Non-Violence is all about revolution.
Non-Violence is all about neutralising violence.
Non-Violence is all about putting an end to violence.
Non-Violence is all about creating a new mentality.

Non-Violence acts as a mirror to those that use violence.
Non-Violence acts as a template for a new behaviour.
Non-Violence acts as a cultural shift.
Non-Violence acts as a new paradigm.
Non-Violence acts as a model for a new world.
Non-Violence acts as a new way to exist.
Non-Violence acts as an example that violence does not need to exist.
Non-Violence acts as an attitude that violent cannot be tolerated.

Imagine a world where violence does not work exist.
I wonder if you can?
You may think that's impossible.
You may think that's the destiny of man.
But I am not one of those.
I believe that one day,
We'll all live in a world as one Human family.
A world of Non-Violence.

"The Don"
22.06.2020

The Death of Humour
(La mort de l'humour)

Some people don't laugh.
Some people don't do laugher.
Don't people like to walk around with a frown.
Some people want to be glum.
Some people want to be gloomy.

But I am not one of them.
I like to laugh.
I like to be funny.
I want to make people laugh.
I want to make people keel over with laughter.

I want to make them piss themselves with laughter.
I want to make them cry with laughter.
I want them to laugh so much it hurts.
And then I want to make them laugh even more.

Laughter is a medicine that cures all ills.
Laughter makes the day shine brightly.
Laughter makes everyone happy.
Laughter brightens everyone's life.
Laughter is free for everyone to have.

Make fun of everything.
Make fun of everyone.
Make fun of all the craziness of this world we're living in.
Make fun of all the absurdities we are fed each day.

Make fun of all the politicians.
Make fun of all the economists.
Make fun of all the Market Forces.
Make fun of Capitalism.

Make fun of money.
Make fun of work.
Make fun of advertisements.
Make fun of greedy ones.

Make fun of the need for fame.
Make for of all those rulers.
Make fun of all those that take things so seriously.
Make fun of religion.

The world is a different place with a grin on your face.
The world laughs with you when you laugh.
The world is a better place when you laugh.
Do not allow The Death of Humour.

I implore everyone to have a sense of humour.
I challenge everyone to laugh.
I throw the gauntlet at your feet.
Do not let humour die.
Do not stand idly by a watch the Death of Humour.

(La mort de l'humour)
The Death of Humour

"The Don"
22.06.2020

Porno

Porno just doesn't do it for me anymore.
It used to excite me.
But now it's just boring.
It's the same old thing.
Have I become a boring old fart?

Or has porno lost its magic?

I used to get very excited.
It used to turn me on.
It was so naughty.
To see what was going on.
But now it's become so predictable.
Porno's lost its zing.

It was explicit.
It was illicit.
It was wild.
It was HOT.
It was illegal.
I used to Lo♥e Porno.

The porn sites are now all the same.
There is no more excitement.
It's become all the same.
There's Pornhub which seems to rule cyberspace.
Porno has lost its titillation.

Maybe it's just me?
Have I become jaded?
What once I found arousing.
Is now simply passé.
Porno is now boring.

It's no longer sexy.
It's no longer erotic.
It's no longer titillating.
It's no longer exciting.
It's no longer arousing.
Porno has become just another thing.

Maybe it's the Internet?
Maybe I've seen it all before?
Maybe it's overexposure?
Maybe it's commercialism?
Maybe it's because I've become old?
Porno doesn't do it for me anymore.

I haven't given up on it though.
I try to get excited.
I try to find something that ignites my fire.
Like it did before.
Porno is not the same, like in those days of yore.

I give shlong a really good workout.
I rub it up & down whilst watching a good fuck.
I like it all, vaginal, anal, DP, blowjob, gonzo, POV, cumswapping,
girl on girl, gangbangs, teen, bizarre, old fucks young, bondage.
The list goes on & on.
But after a while I gave up.
Porno has gone cold.

It's just not the same as hugging a person.
Making Lo♥e instead of just fucking.
Of real passion & desire.
It's way better than that fake one, called Porno.
It's better to make Lo♥e to someone you desire.
Someone that REALLY turns you on & stokes your sexual fire!

I used to Lo♥e Porno.

"The Don"
23.06.2020

The Thinker
(Il Pensatore)

I think.
That's all do.
I don't do anything.
Just think.
'Cause, I'm *The Thinker*.

"I think, therefore I am!"
Descartes said that.
And that's what I do.
I think therefore, I exist.
'Cause, I'm *The Thinker*.

I just walk about.
I do nothing else.
I sometimes sit.
But I think all day.
'Cause, I'm *The Thinker*.

I think at night.
I think even when I sleep.
I never stop.
It can be stressful sometimes.
'Cause, I'm *The Thinker*.

And what do I think about?
You may be wandering?
I think about everything & anything.
Whatever crosses my mind.
'Cause, I'm *The Thinker*.

I think about the state of the world.
I think about the Future.
I think about philosophical questions.
Like the nature of existence & Death.
'Cause, I'm *The Thinker*.

I think about science.
I think about technology.
I think about wars.
I think about the inhumanity of Man.
'Cause, I'm *The Thinker*.

"What conclusions have I come to?" You may ask.
What have I achieved with all this thinking?
What have I created?
What have I done?
'Cause, I'm *The Thinker*.

Absolutely nothing tangible.
Absolutely nothing concrete.
Absolutely necessary though.
Absolutely thinking comes first before action.
I'm *The Thinker*.

One must think before one acts.
One must think before one jumps.
One must think before on decides.
One must think before one commits.
That's why, I'm *The Thinker*.

But now, I have learnt my lesson.
What do I think about?
Absolutely nothing.
I have no thoughts.
I am thoughtless.

I have no mind.
I am mindless.
I have no brain.
I am brainless.
I am *The Thinker* without a mind.

I have no use.
I am useless.
I have no imagination.
I am Imaginationless.
I am *The Thinker* without, imagination.

Thinking only brings you trouble.
Thinking only brings you suffering.
Thinking only brings you problems.
I have stopped thinking.
I am *The Thinker*, that doesn't think.

"The Don"
23.06.2020

Revolution No. 9

You say you want a revolution.
You say you want to change the Constitution.
You say it's evolution.
You say that's the solution.
You say that you've come to that conclusion.
You say you want restitution.
You say you want absolution.
You say you want resolution.
You say it's our obligation.
You say you want to change the institution.
You say you've got information.
You say it'll change the nation.
You say it's due to stagnation.
You say it's all in formation.
You say it's the situation.
You say it's subjection.
You say it's self-flagellation.
You say it's humiliation.
You say that we have wake up from this hibernation.
You say you've got a congregation.
You say you're the leader of "The Concentration".
You say that you're part of an organisation.
You say that you've made a penetration.

You say you're gonna establish a new orientation.
You say that we won't live under subjugation.
You say that it'll be a new orientation.
You say that it'll be a new world without frustration.
You say it's a liberation.
You say I'm invited to the ordination.
You say that you are the new "Co-ordination".
You say you have brought salvation.
You say there's gonna be a high celebration.
You say it's your inauguration.

You say you won't tolerate any insubordination.
You say there'll be incarceration.
You say there'll be no communication.
You say this is your new Administration.
You say you'll rule with total orchestration.
You say of your opposition, there'll be total eradication.
You say under your leadership, there'll be total unification.
You say you're the supreme Goverration.
You say you're the supreme deification.

I say, we need Revolution No. 10.

"The Don"
24.06.2020

Existence

It's a conundrum.
It's a mystery.
What bus the meaning of our lives?
Why are we here?
What is our purpose?
What is it all about?
This thing called Life?
What is this thing called Existence?

There are many theories of course.
There are many explanations.
There are many so called *"Truths"*.
There are many philosophies.
There are many religions.
There are many paths.
There are many *"Schools of Thought"*.
To try to explain our Existence.

Is the life after Death?
Is there an "Afterlife"?
Is there a God?
Is there a Heaven?
Is there a Hell?
Is there a Devil?
Is there spiritual realm?
Is there a reason for our Existence?

Is there a reason?
For all our suffering?
For all our struggles?
For all our arguments?
For all our battles?
For all our perseverance?
For all our accumulations?
For all our Existence?

We study hard.
We get a job.
We go to work.
We hate our work.
We work for the rest of our lives.
We have friends.
We maybe even experience Lo♥e, if we're lucky.
We live for our Existence.

We get old.
We get worn out.
We start to lose our minds.
We start to lose our health.
We start to fall apart.
We start die a slow & ceaseless death.
We start to die from the moment we are born.
We are dying & this is our Existence.

These struggles are not necessary.
This searching for answers is ultimately futile.
If there is a God, the jokes on us.
To be given Life with an expiry date.
There is no great answer.
There is no great Truth.
There is no great purpose.
For our Existence on this Earth.

Accept this fact & it all starts to make sense.
Take each day as it comes & fun all ng the way.
We know where we're all going.
So why struggle & fight.
Accept our destination.
Accept our fate.
Enjoy each moment as if it is your last.
Because it might very well be.
This is all that our Existence is.

There's no meaning for our Existence.
There doesn't have to be one.
It's just that we are looking for an answer.
When there isn't one.
We die & that's a fact.
We die & that is that.
I know it's crazy.
I know it doesn't make any sense.
But just accept that this is our Existence.

Existence

"The Don"
24.06.2020

Fuckability

Do you have the "it" factor?
Do you have the secret?
Do you have "Power of Lo♥e"?
Do you have "animal magnetism"?
Do you have the "Powers of Seduction"?

Do you have **Fuckability**?

Don't be sad if you don't.
There's nothing you can do about.
Either you have or you don't.
That's all there is about it.
Some people do & some people don't.
Not everyone has the power of **Fuckability**.

You'd know if you've got it.
You'd know if you don't.
It's a mysterious power.
It makes you "different".
It makes you "special".
It gives you more desirable.
It makes irresistible from the rest.
If you have the special gift of **Fuckability**.

It makes you irresistible.
It makes you attractive.
It drives people to want you, again & again.
It makes them lose control.
It makes them become infatuated.
It makes them want you right there & then.
It makes them desire your sexuality.
It is all about your **Fuckability**.

Don't fight it.
There is nothing you can do about it.
Some say it's a gift from God himself.
Some say it's "Black Magic".
Some say "you are the work of the Devil".
Those that fear your power.
For secretly they want it.
They wish they had it to.
The power of **Fuckability**.

It can happen anytime.
It can happen any place.
It can happen just walking down the street.
It can happen sitting at a café having a ristretto.
It can happen on a train.
It can happen on a bus.
It can at the beach.
It can happen late at night.
It respects no bounds, this is **Fuckability**.

But you this power wisely.
It's so easy to abuse.
To become so arrogant.
To lose sight of your humanity.
To treat people like objects.
Just for the sake of your sexuality.
Just the sake of your own selfish pleasures.
Your selfish appetites & desires.
You lose the ability to feel.
This is the price one pays for this power.
The power of **Fuckability**.

"The Don"
25.06.2020

The Music Inside My Head

(La musique dans ma tête)

It's everywhere.
It's all around you.
It's in the you breathe.
It's in the wind you feel.
It's in the light you see.
It's a part of Nature.
It's in everything
It's inside you.
It's the music inside my head.

Feel is its rhythm.
Feel its beat.
Feel its melody.
So pure & sweet.
Once it's inside you.
Don't let get out.
It's a flame that burns brightly.
Inside you very soul.
The music inside my head.

It's like having a jukebox inside your brain.
In sunshine or in rain.
Through good times & in bad.
It just keeps on playing.
It never stops.
This is the "House Band".
This is the music inside my head.

It's playing when I wake in the morning.
It's playing when I go sleep at night.
It's playing when I go about my day.
It's playing both day & night.
It's playing whatever song I chose.
It's playing even now.
It's playing the music inside my head.

I am never lonely.
I am never sad.
I'm always ready to sing.
I'm always ready to dance.
I'm ready to dance right now.
I'm ready even though I'm in bed.
I'm ready, 'cause the music is inside my head.

I don't want it to ever stop.
In fact, I don't think it ever will.
This band had set shop.
It looks like it's here to stay.
It's a permanent arrangement.
It'll keep on playing until I'm Dead.
It'll probably still keep playing beyond it as well.
This music inside my head.

"The Don"
25.06.2020

Desire

What do you want?
Is it money?
Is it power?
Is it fame?
Is it sex?
Is it beauty?
Is it creativity?
Is it good looks?
Is it bad looks?
Is it to travel?
Is it to have a house?
Is it spiritual?
Is it happiness?
Is it to feel?
Is it imagination?
Is it good health?
Is it immortality?
Is it to meet God?
Is it to have a "Religious Experience"?
Is it to have an orgasm?
Is it to have an erection?
Is to attain "Enlightenment"?
Is is to meet an "Alien"?
Is it have an "original thought"?
Is it to have any thoughts at all?
Is it to think?
Is it to stop thinking?

Is it to die?
Is to never die.
Is it to live?
Is it to see?
Is to have pleasure?
Is to have fun?
Is it to laugh?
Is it to have a sense of humour?
Is it to have large breasts?
Is to have a huge butt?
Is it to be tall?
Is it to have an enormous cock?
Is it to have play guitar?
Is to sing like the birds?
Is it to fly?
Is it to swim with the dolphins?
Is it to be slim?
Is it to be handsome?
Is it to be a movie star?
Is it to be a supermodel?
Is it to be the Devil?
Is it go to Heaven?
Is it to go to Hell?
Is it to faith?
Is it to have peace?
Is it to have war?
Is it to be Lo♥ed?
Is it to Lo♥e someone?
Is it to Lo♥e?
What do you Desire?

"The Don"
25.06.2020

Imagination

(Immaginazione)

Someone once told me long ago,
"Imagination to Power!"
No truer words have ever been spoken.
For without *"Imagination"*, there would be nothing.
Nothing at all.

Imagination is the tool to unlock the in foreseen.
Imagination is the key to see The Future.
Imagination is the basis of all creativity.
Imagination is the portal into other *"Realities"*.

Without it we could not think.
There would be no new solutions.
There would be new developments.
There would be new pathways to follow.

There would be no new ways of thinking.
There would be no new ways of seeing.
There would be no new ways of being.
There would be nothing.

There is Imagination everywhere.
There is Imagination in everyone.
There is Imagination in Nature.
There is Imagination in you.

Nature is an extraordinary thing.
Nature is full of wild Imagination.
Nature has imagined amazing things.
Nature is bursting with Imagination.

Don't say that, "you have no Imagination".
You know that isn't true.
It's deep inside you.
You just don't know what to do.

Maybe, you have told that you lack Imagination.
That you don't have Imagination.
Don't believe this at all 'cause it's not true.
Just open the door inside you called Imagination.

Allow Imagination to run freely.
Allow it to run unconstrained.
Allow it to go crazy.
Allow it to go insane.

Imagination knows what to do.
Imagination can do the rest.
Imagination knows what is best.
Imagination can pass any test.

Do not put barriers to Imagination.
Do not restrain or fence it in.
Do not put it in box as a prisoner.
Do not keep it locked up.

Imagination is the key.
Imagination is the door.
Imagination is the portal.
Imagination is the Power.

Imagination to Power.
Imagination for happiness.
Imagination for creativity.
Imagination for Life.

"The Don"
25.06.2020

Poetic Politicians

(Politici Poetici)

Why do most politicians have to be,
lawyers?
Economists?
Bankers?
Developers?
Financiers?
Or have a background in these areas?

Why can we have politicians who are artists?
Poets?
Writers?
Actors?
Singers?
Comedians?
Clowns?
Unemployed?
Students?
Women?
Aboriginal?
Homosexual?

Why do people from these backgrounds not become politicians?
Why is emphasis on the economy so important?
Isn't quality of life more than just economics?
Aren't there other areas that are just as important if not more important?

Areas like,
The Arts,
The environment,
Science,
Education,
Health.

There was only one politician that I know of that was like this.
His name was *Vaclav Havel*.
You may not know of him.

You may not have heard of his name.
But he was a play writer & an intellectual.
He was a *"Revolutionary & a Dissident"*.
He was the leader of the *"Purple Revolution"*.

He was put in goal many times.
Spent many years in prison.
But he led a *"Non-Violent Revolution"*.
And become the President of a Nation.
He became President of the newly formed Czech Republic in 1989.

When Czechoslovakia separated into two separate Nations,
The Czech Republic & Slovakia.
It was a peaceful separation.
No blood was shed at all.
A negotiated agreement conducted by a playwriter.

It shows that it can be done!
And successfully too.
Don't listen those that say they have all the answers.
Because we know it isn't true.

We need a new way of thinking in political affairs.
A new set of eyes to see with.
Not the old ideas that is constantly being regurgitated.
We need *Poetic Politicians*.

Let's throw the old paradigms out the window.
Let's throw out those old, mouldy economic theories too
Let's bring in the new thinking, of art, culture & science.
Let's usher in the new dawn of the *Poetic Politicians*.

"The Don"
25.06.2020

Sex Bomb

(Bombe Sexuelle)

You're a real wild one, wild one, wild one, wild one.
Ooh, yeah, you're a wild one.
You're a wild child.
You make me break loose.
You make me go crazy.
You keep me swingin' baby,
'Cause you're a real wild child.
Wild child, wild child, wild child.
You're my sex bomb, sex bomb.
And baby you sure can turn me on.

You're a real wild one & you like wild fun
We live in a world gone crazy.
Everything seems so hazy.
You like to lay naked under the Sun.
You're a wild child baby.
You drive me crazy.
In you're wild, wild way.
You live for pleasure & that's okay
You like to take drugs, you like to have sex.
You're a real wild one, wild one, wild one.
You're my sex bomb, sex bomb.
And baby you sure can turn me on.

You were born to be wild.
You were born to take me for a ride.
You make my motor run hot.
You've got the lot.
You know just what to do.
What the hell baby, you can do that too?
You never know when to stop.
You keep on going forever until you make me drop.
You then say, *"Come on baby, is that all you've got?"*
"I want more, more, more, I want the lot!"

You're my sex bomb, sex bomb.
And baby you sure can turn me on.

'Cause you were born to be wild.
You're a real wild child.
You're my sex bomb, sex bomb.
And baby you sure can turn me on.

Your name is *"Juicy Julie"*.
You set me on fire, truly.
You're my heart's desire.
You're all that I require.
You've got a body to die for.
You're super sexy & much more.
You're my sex machine.
You're my sex bomb, sex bomb.
And baby you sure can turn me on.

She's Oriental.
She's continental.
But she's definitely not sentimental.
She's Eurasian.
She's Caucasian.
She's Scandinavian.
She's Pacific Islander.
But she's definitely not shy when it comes being tender.
You're my sex bomb, sex bomb.
And baby you sure can turn me on.

You're a *Real Wild Child*.
You're a *Real Rebel Child*.
You're a *Real Hot Babe*.
You're a *Real "Wild Honey"*.
You're a *Real "Honeypot"*.
You're a *Real "Lo ♥e Box"*.
You're a *Real "Sugar Jar"*.
You're a *Real "Pussy Kat"*.
You're a *Real "Muff Pie"*.
You're a *Real "Glory Tunnel"*.
You're a *Real Sex Bomb*.

You're my sex bomb, sex bomb.
And baby you sure can turn me on.
You're my sex bomb, sex bomb.
And baby you sure can turn me on.

You've got a body that taught & terrific.
I'm sure, baby that you're from the South Pacific.
You've got legs that reach up to Heaven.
They wrap around my face & count up to se7en.
When you squeeze me tight, you turn off my lights.
You leave me breathless & falling from great heights.

You're my sex bomb, sex bomb.
And baby you sure can turn me on.

You're so juicy & ripe like a peach.
You're so tasty, I suck you like a leach.
You're so sexy, you're so hot.
You're horny, you're like a *"sexbot"*.
You're body's like a snake, so smooth delicious.
You're so beautiful, you make me almost turn religious.

You're my sex bomb, sex bomb.
And baby you sure can turn me on.

"Sex bomb, sex bomb, you're a sex bomb uh, huh
You can give it to me when I need to come along (give it to me).
Sex bomb, sex bomb, you're my sex bomb.
And baby you can turn me on (baby you can turn me on).
(You know what you're doing to me don't you, I know you do)".

"Sex bomb, sex bomb, you're my sex bomb uh, huh.
You can give it to me when I need to come along.
Sex bomb, sex bomb, you're my sex bomb.
And baby you can turn me on (turn me on).
Sex bomb, sex bomb, you're my sex bomb (sex bomb).
You can give it to me when I need to come along.
Sex bomb, sex bomb, you're my sex bomb.
And baby you can turn me on."

"Sex bomb sex bomb you're my sex bomb.
And baby you can turn me on (turn me on).
And baby you can turn me on (turn me on).
Baby you can turn me on (turn me on).
Ooh baby, you can turn me on (turn me on).
Baby you can turn me on, ooh (turn me on).
Baby you can turn me on.
Well, baby you can turn me on."

"The Don"
25.06.2020

Happy Days

"Those were "Happy Days", you hear people say.
But, were they really happy?
Reminiscence is a funny thing.
It's like looking through "rose coloured" glasses.
You don't see the "Real" thing.

It's a distortion.
It's not everything.
It's been filtered.
It's had parts removed.
It's had all the "negativity" taken out.
It's had all "trauma" exorcised.
It's been sanitised.

Where is the angst?
Where is the pain?
Where is the suffering.
Where is the hurt?
Where is the abuse?
Where is the violence?
Where is the rejection?
Where is the loneliness?
Where is the anger?
Where is the disappointment?

"Those were not the days", my friend.
We didn't "laugh & sing", all the time.
We didn't "dance & have fun", every day.
We didn't "live forever & a day".
It wasn't "the life we chose".
We didn't, "think we would ever lose".
It was like "Mary Hopkin's" sang in that song.
Those were not the days.

They were not days of all sunshine.
There was a lot of rain too.
They were not days of all singing.
There were many days of crying too.
They were not days of all fun.
There were many days of sadness too.
They were not days of all Lo♥e.
There were many days of hate too.

Reminiscing is a funny thing.
It's not "Real".

Don't be fooled by it.
Don't be caught up by its illusion.
Don't long for days long gone.
Don't repurpose the Past.
Don't make it something it wasn't.

Live in the "Moment".
Enjoy the "Here & Now".
This is "Reality".
That's all there is my friend.
These are your "Real" happy days.

Happy Days

"The Don"
27.06.2020

www.ingramcontent.com/pod-product-compliance
Lightning Source LLC
Chambersburg PA
CBHW041501010526
44107CB00049B/1615